Today, I Choose Gratitude

Choose an attitude of gratitude

Dianne B. Terry

Réalta Publications
Shawnee, KS

Published by Réalta Publications in 2018
First Edition; First printing

Design and writing by Dianne Terry

ISBN: 978-0-9600417-4-9

How to Use This Journal

Why should I start this journal?

The purpose of the journal is to help you on your journey to make gratitude your new attitude. Each day of the year, we should be grateful for things we often take for granted. When you take a few minutes to write down what you are thankful for each day, you will begin to see a change in how you view life.

What should I write about?

Perhaps you took a walk in the park and saw the most beautiful butterfly or the most industrious bee you've ever seen. What was so remarkable about what you saw? Maybe you are grateful for a person. Why? What does that person mean to you? Did you receive something you weren't expecting? How did it make you feel? Has something happened that changed your life?

There really are so many things for which we can be grateful.

How should I start this journal?

Start with the first week in the journal. If your first day in the journal is Monday, start with Monday of week 1. If the first day is Thursday, start with Thursday of week 1. There are a couple of extra weeks included at the end of this journal in case you need them.

What do I need to know about the journal?

A new quote is provided each week. At the end of the week, write down any additional things you've discovered in your journey. Be creative! Have fun.

How to Use This Journal—cont'd

If you have writer's block or run out of things to write about, I've listed a few questions below that might jog your memory.

- Name one of your favorite songs when you were growing up.
- Who was your best friend in school?
- Who is your best friend now?
- What was your first pet's name?
- What was your biggest accomplishment last year?
- What has been your biggest accomplishment in your professional life?
- What has been your biggest accomplishment in your personal life?
- What is your favorite memory of your father or stepfather?
- What is your favorite memory of your mother or stepmother?
- What family tradition do your treasure most during the holidays?
- What is your favorite vacation? When was the last time you were there?
- What is your favorite holiday movie?
- What is your favorite meal?
- Describe your favorite smell.
- When was the last time you did something just for you? What was it? How did it make you feel?
- What do you like about yourself?
- What do others like most about you?
- Where was the most unusual place you've ever visited?
- Is there someone you've lost contact with? How can you get in touch? Why were they important in your life?
- Who has made the biggest impact in your life? Why?
- Have you changed anyone's life for the better? Who was it? How?

Sometimes we should express our gratitude for the small and simple things like the scent of the rain, the taste of your favorite food, or the sound of a loved one's voice.

Joseph B. Wirthlin

Monday

Date: _____

_____
_____
_____
_____
_____
_____
_____
_____
_____

Tuesday

Date: _____

_____
_____
_____
_____
_____
_____
_____
_____
_____
_____

Wednesday

Date: _____

_____
_____
_____
_____
_____
_____
_____
_____
_____

Thursday

Date: _____

_____
_____
_____
_____
_____
_____
_____
_____
_____
_____

Friday

Date: _____

_____
_____
_____
_____
_____
_____
_____
_____
_____

Saturday

Date: _____

_____
_____
_____
_____
_____
_____
_____
_____

Sunday

Date: _____

_____
_____
_____
_____
_____
_____
_____
_____

Additional Thoughts About This Week?

_____
_____
_____
_____
_____
_____
_____
_____

Week 2

> Gratitude is the inward feeling of kindness received.
> Thankfulness is the natural impulse to express that feeling.
> Thanksgiving is the following of that impulse.
> Henry Van Dyke

Monday

Date: _____

_____
_____
_____
_____
_____
_____
_____
_____
_____
_____

Tuesday

Date: _____

_____
_____
_____
_____
_____
_____
_____
_____
_____
_____

Wednesday

Date: _____

_____
_____
_____
_____
_____
_____
_____
_____
_____

Thursday

Date: _____

_____
_____
_____
_____
_____
_____
_____
_____
_____
_____
_____

Friday

Date: _____

_____
_____
_____
_____
_____
_____
_____
_____
_____

Saturday

Date: _____

_____
_____
_____
_____
_____
_____
_____
_____
_____

Sunday

Date: _____

_____
_____
_____
_____
_____
_____
_____
_____
_____

Additional Thoughts About This Week?

_____
_____
_____
_____
_____
_____
_____
_____

Week 3

> *Happiness cannot be traveled to, owned, earned, worn or consumed. Happiness is the spiritual experience of living every minute with love, grace, and gratitude.*
>
> Denis Waitley

Monday

Date: _____

_____
_____
_____
_____
_____
_____
_____
_____

Tuesday

Date: _____

_____
_____
_____
_____
_____
_____
_____
_____

Wednesday

Date: _____

_____
_____
_____
_____
_____
_____
_____
_____
_____

Thursday

Date: _____

_____
_____
_____
_____
_____
_____
_____
_____
_____
_____

Friday

Date: _____

_____
_____
_____
_____
_____
_____
_____
_____

Saturday

Date: _____

_____
_____
_____
_____
_____
_____
_____
_____
_____

Sunday

Date: _____

_____
_____
_____
_____
_____
_____
_____
_____
_____

Additional Thoughts About This Week?

_____
_____
_____
_____
_____
_____
_____
_____
_____

I don't have to chase extraordinary moments to find happiness - it's right in front of me if I'm paying attention and practicing gratitude.

Brene Brown

Monday

Date: _____

_____

_____

_____

_____

_____

_____

_____

_____

_____

Tuesday

Date: _____

_____

_____

_____

_____

_____

_____

_____

_____

_____

Wednesday

Date: _____

_____
_____
_____
_____
_____
_____
_____
_____
_____

Thursday

Date: _____

_____
_____
_____
_____
_____
_____
_____
_____
_____
_____

Friday

Date: _____

_____
_____
_____
_____
_____
_____
_____
_____
_____

Saturday

Date: _____

_____
_____
_____
_____
_____
_____
_____
_____
_____
_____

Sunday

Date: _____

_____
_____
_____
_____
_____
_____
_____
_____
_____
_____

Additional Thoughts About This Week?

_____
_____
_____
_____
_____
_____
_____
_____

America's fighting men and women sacrifice much to ensure that our great nation stays free. We owe a debt of gratitude to the soldiers that have paid the ultimate price for this cause, as well as for those who are blessed enough to return from the battlefield unscathed.

Allen Boyd

Monday

Date: _____

_____
_____
_____
_____
_____
_____
_____
_____
_____

Tuesday

Date: _____

_____
_____
_____
_____
_____
_____
_____
_____

Wednesday

Date: _____

_____

_____

_____

_____

_____

_____

_____

_____

_____

Thursday

Date: _____

_____

_____

_____

_____

_____

_____

_____

_____

_____

Friday

Date: _____

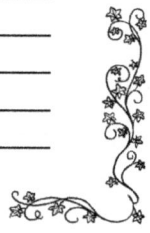

_____

_____

_____

_____

_____

_____

_____

_____

_____

Saturday

Date: _____

_____
_____
_____
_____
_____
_____
_____

Sunday

Date: _____

_____
_____
_____
_____
_____
_____
_____

Additional Thoughts About This Week?

_____
_____
_____
_____
_____
_____

Week 6

> "Grateful" is a small word to express my gratitude, as God has blessed me with so many opportunities to restart my life.
>
> Adnam Sami

Monday

Date: _____

_____
_____
_____
_____
_____
_____
_____
_____
_____
_____

Tuesday

Date: _____

_____
_____
_____
_____
_____
_____
_____
_____
_____
_____

Wednesday

Date: _____

_____
_____
_____
_____
_____
_____
_____
_____
_____

Thursday

Date: _____

_____
_____
_____
_____
_____
_____
_____
_____
_____
_____
_____

Friday

Date: _____

_____
_____
_____
_____
_____
_____
_____
_____
_____

Saturday

Date: _____

_____
_____
_____
_____
_____
_____
_____
_____
_____
_____

Sunday

Date: _____

_____
_____
_____
_____
_____
_____
_____
_____
_____
_____

Additional Thoughts About This Week?

_____
_____
_____
_____
_____
_____
_____
_____
_____

Week 7

> *Opportunities are like sunrises.*
> *If you wait too long, you miss them.*
> William Arthur Ward

Monday

Date: _____

_____
_____
_____
_____
_____
_____
_____
_____
_____

Tuesday

Date: _____

_____
_____
_____
_____
_____
_____
_____
_____
_____

Wednesday

Date: _____

_____

_____

_____

_____

_____

_____

_____

_____

_____

Thursday

Date: _____

_____

_____

_____

_____

_____

_____

_____

_____

_____

_____

Friday

Date: _____

_____

_____

_____

_____

_____

_____

_____

_____

_____

_____

Saturday

Date: _____

_____
_____
_____
_____
_____
_____
_____
_____
_____

Sunday

Date: _____

_____
_____
_____
_____
_____
_____
_____
_____
_____

Additional Thoughts About This Week?

_____
_____
_____
_____
_____
_____
_____
_____

When you have balance in your life, work becomes an entirely different experience. There is a passion that moves you to a whole new level of fulfillment and gratitude, and that's when you can do your best . . . For yourself and for others.

Cara Delevingne

Monday

Date: _____

_____
_____
_____
_____
_____
_____
_____
_____
_____
_____

Tuesday

Date: _____

_____
_____
_____
_____
_____
_____
_____
_____
_____
_____

Wednesday

Date: _____

_____
_____
_____
_____
_____
_____
_____
_____
_____

Thursday

Date: _____

_____
_____
_____
_____
_____
_____
_____
_____
_____
_____

Friday

Date: _____

_____
_____
_____
_____
_____
_____
_____
_____
_____

Saturday

Date: _____

_____
_____
_____
_____
_____
_____
_____
_____
_____
_____

Sunday

Date: _____

_____
_____
_____
_____
_____
_____
_____
_____
_____
_____

Additional Thoughts About This Week?

_____
_____
_____
_____
_____
_____
_____
_____
_____

> *The discipline of gratitude is the explicit effort to*
> *acknowledge that all I am and have is given to me*
> *as a gift of love, a gift to be celebrated with joy.*
> Henri Nouwen

Monday

Date: _____

_____
_____
_____
_____
_____
_____
_____
_____
_____
_____

Tuesday

Date: _____

_____
_____
_____
_____
_____
_____
_____
_____
_____

Wednesday

Date: _____

_____
_____
_____
_____
_____
_____
_____
_____
_____

Thursday

Date: _____

_____
_____
_____
_____
_____
_____
_____
_____
_____

Friday

Date: _____

_____
_____
_____
_____
_____
_____
_____
_____
_____

Saturday

Date: _____

_____
_____
_____
_____
_____
_____
_____
_____
_____

Sunday

Date: _____

_____
_____
_____
_____
_____
_____
_____
_____
_____

Additional Thoughts About This Week?

_____
_____
_____
_____
_____
_____
_____
_____
_____

Week 10

> *Nature's beauty is a gift that cultivates appreciation and gratitude.*
> *Louie Schwartzberg*

Monday

Date: _____

_____
_____
_____
_____
_____
_____
_____
_____
_____

Tuesday

Date: _____

_____
_____
_____
_____
_____
_____
_____
_____
_____

Wednesday

Date: _____

_____
_____
_____
_____
_____
_____
_____
_____
_____

Thursday

Date: _____

_____
_____
_____
_____
_____
_____
_____
_____
_____
_____

Friday

Date: _____

_____
_____
_____
_____
_____
_____
_____
_____

Saturday

Date: _____

_____
_____
_____
_____
_____
_____
_____
_____
_____

Sunday

Date: _____

_____
_____
_____
_____
_____
_____
_____
_____
_____

Additional Thoughts About This Week?

_____
_____
_____
_____
_____
_____
_____
_____

At times our own light goes out and is rekindled by a spark from another person. Each of us has cause to think with deep gratitude of those who have lighted the flame within us.

Albert Schweitzer

Monday   Date: _____

_____
_____
_____
_____
_____
_____
_____
_____
_____
_____

Tuesday   Date: _____

_____
_____
_____
_____
_____
_____
_____
_____
_____

Wednesday

Date: _____

_____
_____
_____
_____
_____
_____
_____
_____
_____

Thursday

Date: _____

_____
_____
_____
_____
_____
_____
_____
_____
_____
_____
_____

Friday

Date: _____

_____
_____
_____
_____
_____
_____
_____
_____
_____
_____

Saturday

Date: _____

_____
_____
_____
_____
_____
_____
_____
_____

Sunday

Date: _____

_____
_____
_____
_____
_____
_____
_____
_____

Additional Thoughts About This Week?

_____
_____
_____
_____
_____
_____
_____
_____

A warm smile is the universal language of kindness.
William Arthur Ward

Monday

Date: _____

_____
_____
_____
_____
_____
_____
_____
_____
_____
_____

Tuesday

Date: _____

_____
_____
_____
_____
_____
_____
_____
_____
_____
_____

Wednesday

Date: _____

_____
_____
_____
_____
_____
_____
_____
_____

Thursday

Date: _____

_____
_____
_____
_____
_____
_____
_____
_____
_____
_____

Friday

Date: _____

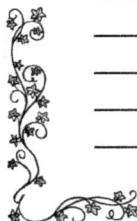

_____
_____
_____
_____
_____
_____
_____
_____
_____

Saturday

Date: _____

_____
_____
_____
_____
_____
_____
_____
_____
_____

Sunday

Date: _____

_____
_____
_____
_____
_____
_____
_____
_____
_____

Additional Thoughts About This Week?

_____
_____
_____
_____
_____
_____
_____
_____

Week 13

Every day, I am blessed by the goodness in our country
and the kindness and the generosity of the American people.
We share a deep love for this place and a gratutude
for the contributions we each make.

Cary Kennedy

Monday

Date: _____

_____
_____
_____
_____
_____
_____
_____
_____
_____
_____
_____

Tuesday

Date: _____

_____
_____
_____
_____
_____
_____
_____
_____
_____
_____
_____

Wednesday

Date: _____

_____
_____
_____
_____
_____
_____
_____
_____
_____
_____

Thursday

Date: _____

_____
_____
_____
_____
_____
_____
_____
_____
_____
_____

Friday

Date: _____

_____
_____
_____
_____
_____
_____
_____
_____
_____
_____

Saturday

Date: _____

_____
_____
_____
_____
_____
_____
_____
_____

Sunday

Date: _____

_____
_____
_____
_____
_____
_____
_____
_____

Additional Thoughts About This Week?

_____
_____
_____
_____
_____
_____
_____
_____

Gratitude unlocks the fullness of life. It turns what we have into enough, and more. It turns denial into acceptance, chaos to order, confusion to clarity. It can turn a meal into a feast, a house into a home, a stranger into a friend.

Melody Beattie

Monday

Date: _____

_____
_____
_____
_____
_____
_____
_____
_____

Tuesday

Date: _____

_____
_____
_____
_____
_____
_____
_____
_____

Wednesday

Date: _____

_____
_____
_____
_____
_____
_____
_____
_____
_____

Thursday

Date: _____

_____
_____
_____
_____
_____
_____
_____
_____
_____
_____

Friday

Date: _____

_____
_____
_____
_____
_____
_____
_____
_____

Saturday

Date: _____

_____
_____
_____
_____
_____
_____
_____
_____
_____
_____

Sunday

Date: _____

_____
_____
_____
_____
_____
_____
_____
_____
_____
_____

Additional Thoughts About This Week?

_____
_____
_____
_____
_____
_____
_____
_____
_____

Week 15

> *The simple act of saying "thank you" is a demonstration of gratitude in response to an experience that was meaningful to a customer or citizen.*
> Siman Mainwaring

Monday

Date: _____

_____
_____
_____
_____
_____
_____
_____
_____
_____
_____

Tuesday

Date: _____

_____
_____
_____
_____
_____
_____
_____
_____
_____
_____

Wednesday

Date: _____

_____

_____

_____

_____

_____

_____

_____

_____

Thursday

Date: _____

_____

_____

_____

_____

_____

_____

_____

_____

_____

_____

Friday

Date: _____

_____

_____

_____

_____

_____

_____

_____

_____

_____

Saturday

Date: _____

_____
_____
_____
_____
_____
_____
_____
_____
_____

Sunday

Date: _____

_____
_____
_____
_____
_____
_____
_____
_____
_____
_____

Additional Thoughts About This Week?

_____
_____
_____
_____
_____
_____
_____
_____

Week 16

> *It is through gratitude for the present moment that the spiritual dimension of life opens up.*
> *Eckhart Tolle*

Monday

Date: _____

_____

_____

_____

_____

_____

_____

_____

_____

_____

_____

Tuesday

Date: _____

_____

_____

_____

_____

_____

_____

_____

_____

_____

Wednesday

Date: _____

_____

_____

_____

_____

_____

_____

_____

_____

Thursday

Date: _____

_____

_____

_____

_____

_____

_____

_____

_____

_____

Friday

Date: _____

_____

_____

_____

_____

_____

_____

_____

_____

_____

Saturday

Date: _____

_____
_____
_____
_____
_____
_____
_____
_____

Sunday

Date: _____

_____
_____
_____
_____
_____
_____
_____
_____

Additional Thoughts About This Week?

_____
_____
_____
_____
_____
_____
_____
_____

Giving is an expression of gratitude for our blessings.
Laura Arrillaga-Andreessen

Monday

Date: _____

_____
_____
_____
_____
_____
_____
_____
_____
_____

Tuesday

Date: _____

_____
_____
_____
_____
_____
_____
_____
_____
_____

Wednesday

Date: _____

_____

_____

_____

_____

_____

_____

_____

_____

_____

Thursday

Date: _____

_____

_____

_____

_____

_____

_____

_____

_____

_____

_____

Friday

Date: _____

_____

_____

_____

_____

_____

_____

_____

_____

Saturday

Date: _____

_____
_____
_____
_____
_____
_____
_____
_____

Sunday

Date: _____

_____
_____
_____
_____
_____
_____
_____
_____

Additional Thoughts About This Week?

_____
_____
_____
_____
_____
_____
_____
_____

Week 18

> To find gratitude and generosity when you could reasonably find hurt and resentment will surprise you. It will be so surprising because you will see so much of the opposite: people who have much more than others yet who react with anger when one advantage is lost or with resentment when an added gift is denied. Henry B. Eyring

Monday

Date: _____

_____
_____
_____
_____
_____
_____
_____
_____
_____
_____

Tuesday

Date: _____

_____
_____
_____
_____
_____
_____
_____
_____

Wednesday

Date: _____

_____
_____
_____
_____
_____
_____
_____
_____

Thursday

Date: _____

_____
_____
_____
_____
_____
_____
_____
_____
_____

Friday

Date: _____

_____
_____
_____
_____
_____
_____
_____
_____

Saturday

Date: _____

_____
_____
_____
_____
_____
_____
_____
_____
_____

Sunday

Date: _____

_____
_____
_____
_____
_____
_____
_____
_____
_____

Additional Thoughts About This Week?

_____
_____
_____
_____
_____
_____
_____
_____

> *Only I can change my life. No one can do it for me.*
> Carol Burnett

Monday

Date: _____

_____
_____
_____
_____
_____
_____
_____
_____

Tuesday

Date: _____

_____
_____
_____
_____
_____
_____
_____
_____

Wednesday

Date: _____

_____
_____
_____
_____
_____
_____
_____
_____
_____

Thursday

Date: _____

_____
_____
_____
_____
_____
_____
_____
_____
_____
_____
_____

Friday

Date: _____

_____
_____
_____
_____
_____
_____
_____
_____
_____
_____

Saturday

Date: _____

_____
_____
_____
_____
_____
_____
_____
_____
_____

Sunday

Date: _____

_____
_____
_____
_____
_____
_____
_____
_____
_____

Additional Thoughts About This Week?

_____
_____
_____
_____
_____
_____
_____
_____

Week 20

> *Gratitude changes the pangs of memory into a tranquil joy.*
> Dietrich Bonhoeffer

Monday

Date: _____

_____
_____
_____
_____
_____
_____
_____
_____
_____

Tuesday

Date: _____

_____
_____
_____
_____
_____
_____
_____
_____
_____

Wednesday

Date: _____

_____
_____
_____
_____
_____
_____
_____
_____
_____

Thursday

Date: _____

_____
_____
_____
_____
_____
_____
_____
_____
_____
_____

Friday

Date: _____

_____
_____
_____
_____
_____
_____
_____
_____
_____

Saturday

Date: _____

_____
_____
_____
_____
_____
_____
_____
_____
_____
_____

Sunday

Date: _____

_____
_____
_____
_____
_____
_____
_____
_____
_____
_____

Additional Thoughts About This Week?

_____
_____
_____
_____
_____
_____
_____
_____
_____

Week 21

> *Adversity causes some men to break;*
>
> *others to break records.*
>
> *William Arthur Ward*

Monday

Date: _____

_____
_____
_____
_____
_____
_____
_____
_____
_____

Tuesday

Date: _____

_____
_____
_____
_____
_____
_____
_____
_____
_____

Wednesday

Date: _____

_____
_____
_____
_____
_____
_____
_____
_____
_____

Thursday

Date: _____

_____
_____
_____
_____
_____
_____
_____
_____
_____

Friday

Date: _____

_____
_____
_____
_____
_____
_____
_____
_____

Saturday

Date: _____

_____
_____
_____
_____
_____
_____
_____
_____
_____

Sunday

Date: _____

_____
_____
_____
_____
_____
_____
_____
_____
_____

Additional Thoughts About This Week?

_____
_____
_____
_____
_____
_____
_____
_____

Week 22

No one who achieves success does so without acknowledging the help of others. The wise and confident acknowledge this help with gratitude.

Alfred North Whitehead

Monday

Date: _____

_____
_____
_____
_____
_____
_____
_____
_____
_____
_____

Tuesday

Date: _____

_____
_____
_____
_____
_____
_____
_____
_____
_____

Wednesday

Date: _____

_____
_____
_____
_____
_____
_____
_____
_____
_____

Thursday

Date: _____

_____
_____
_____
_____
_____
_____
_____
_____
_____
_____

Friday

Date: _____

_____
_____
_____
_____
_____
_____
_____
_____
_____

Saturday

Date: _____

_____
_____
_____
_____
_____
_____
_____
_____
_____

Sunday

Date: _____

_____
_____
_____
_____
_____
_____
_____
_____
_____

Additional Thoughts About This Week?

_____
_____
_____
_____
_____
_____
_____
_____

Week 23

Gratitude is the sign of noble souls.
Aesop

Monday

Date: _____

_____
_____
_____
_____
_____
_____
_____
_____

Tuesday

Date: _____

_____
_____
_____
_____
_____
_____
_____
_____

Wednesday

Date: _____

_____
_____
_____
_____
_____
_____
_____
_____
_____

Thursday

Date: _____

_____
_____
_____
_____
_____
_____
_____
_____
_____
_____

Friday

Date: _____

_____
_____
_____
_____
_____
_____
_____
_____

Saturday

Date: _____

_____
_____
_____
_____
_____
_____
_____
_____
_____

Sunday

Date: _____

_____
_____
_____
_____
_____
_____
_____
_____
_____

Additional Thoughts About This Week?

_____
_____
_____
_____
_____
_____
_____
_____

For me, every hour is grace. And I feel gratitude in my heart each time I can meet someone and look at his or her smile.
Elie Wiesel

Monday

Date: _____

_____
_____
_____
_____
_____
_____
_____
_____
_____
_____

Tuesday

Date: _____

_____
_____
_____
_____
_____
_____
_____
_____
_____
_____

Wednesday

Date: _____

_____

_____

_____

_____

_____

_____

_____

_____

_____

Thursday

Date: _____

_____

_____

_____

_____

_____

_____

_____

_____

_____

_____

Friday

Date: _____

_____

_____

_____

_____

_____

_____

_____

_____

_____

Saturday

Date: _____

_____
_____
_____
_____
_____
_____
_____
_____
_____

Sunday

Date: _____

_____
_____
_____
_____
_____
_____
_____
_____
_____

Additional Thoughts About This Week?

_____
_____
_____
_____
_____
_____
_____
_____

Week 25

> *Gratitude is riches. Complaint is poverty.*
> *Doris Day*

Monday

Date: _____

_____
_____
_____
_____
_____
_____
_____
_____
_____

Tuesday

Date: _____

_____
_____
_____
_____
_____
_____
_____
_____
_____

Wednesday

Date: _____

_____

_____

_____

_____

_____

_____

_____

_____

_____

Thursday

Date: _____

_____

_____

_____

_____

_____

_____

_____

_____

_____

_____

_____

Friday

Date: _____

_____

_____

_____

_____

_____

_____

_____

_____

_____

Saturday

Date: _____

_____
_____
_____
_____
_____
_____
_____
_____

Sunday

Date: _____

_____
_____
_____
_____
_____
_____
_____
_____
_____

Additional Thoughts About This Week?

_____
_____
_____
_____
_____
_____
_____
_____

Week 26

> *Life is 10% what happens to you*
> *and 90% how you react to it.*
> Charles R. Swindoll

Monday

Date: _____

_____
_____
_____
_____
_____
_____
_____
_____
_____
_____

Tuesday

Date: _____

_____
_____
_____
_____
_____
_____
_____
_____
_____
_____

Wednesday

Date: _____

_____
_____
_____
_____
_____
_____
_____
_____
_____

Thursday

Date: _____

_____
_____
_____
_____
_____
_____
_____
_____
_____
_____

Friday

Date: _____

_____
_____
_____
_____
_____
_____
_____
_____
_____
_____

Saturday

Date: _____

_____
_____
_____
_____
_____
_____
_____
_____
_____
_____

Sunday

Date: _____

_____
_____
_____
_____
_____
_____
_____
_____
_____
_____

Additional Thoughts About This Week?

_____
_____
_____
_____
_____
_____
_____
_____

Week 27

> Gratitude is not only the greatest of virtues,
> but the parent of all the others.
> Marcus Tullius Cicero

Monday

Date: _____

_____
_____
_____
_____
_____
_____
_____
_____
_____

Tuesday

Date: _____

_____
_____
_____
_____
_____
_____
_____
_____

Wednesday

Date: _____

_____
_____
_____
_____
_____
_____
_____
_____
_____

Thursday

Date: _____

_____
_____
_____
_____
_____
_____
_____
_____
_____
_____
_____

Friday

Date: _____

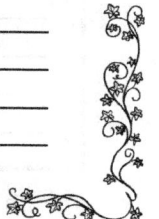

_____
_____
_____
_____
_____
_____
_____
_____
_____

Saturday

Date: _____

_____
_____
_____
_____
_____
_____
_____
_____

Sunday

Date: _____

_____
_____
_____
_____
_____
_____
_____
_____

Additional Thoughts About This Week?

_____
_____
_____
_____
_____
_____
_____
_____

It's wonderful to be grateful. To have that gratitude well out from deep within you and pour out in waves. Once you truly experience this, you will never want to give it up.

Srikumar Rao

Monday

Date: _____

_____
_____
_____
_____
_____
_____
_____
_____
_____

Tuesday

Date: _____

_____
_____
_____
_____
_____
_____
_____
_____
_____

Wednesday

Date: _____

_____

_____

_____

_____

_____

_____

_____

_____

Thursday

Date: _____

_____

_____

_____

_____

_____

_____

_____

_____

_____

Friday

Date: _____

_____

_____

_____

_____

_____

_____

_____

_____

_____

Saturday

Date: _____

_____
_____
_____
_____
_____
_____
_____
_____

Sunday

Date: _____

_____
_____
_____
_____
_____
_____
_____
_____
_____

Additional Thoughts About This Week?

_____
_____
_____
_____
_____
_____
_____

Week 29

> The key to the happy life, it seems, is the good life:
> a life with sustained relationships, challenging work,
> and connections to community.
>
> Paul Bloom

Monday

Date: _____

_____
_____
_____
_____
_____
_____
_____
_____
_____

Tuesday

Date: _____

_____
_____
_____
_____
_____
_____
_____
_____

Wednesday

Date: _____

_____

_____

_____

_____

_____

_____

_____

_____

_____

Thursday

Date: _____

_____

_____

_____

_____

_____

_____

_____

_____

_____

_____

Friday

Date: _____

_____

_____

_____

_____

_____

_____

_____

_____

_____

_____

Saturday

Date: _____

_____
_____
_____
_____
_____
_____
_____
_____

Sunday

Date: _____

_____
_____
_____
_____
_____
_____
_____
_____

Additional Thoughts About This Week?

_____
_____
_____
_____
_____
_____
_____
_____

Week 30

> As we express our gratitude, we must never forget that the highest appreciation is not to utter words, but to live by them.
> John F. Kennedy

Monday

Date: _____

_____

_____

_____

_____

_____

_____

_____

_____

_____

_____

Tuesday

Date: _____

_____

_____

_____

_____

_____

_____

_____

_____

_____

_____

Wednesday

Date: _____

_____
_____
_____
_____
_____
_____
_____
_____

Thursday

Date: _____

_____
_____
_____
_____
_____
_____
_____
_____
_____

Friday

Date: _____

_____
_____
_____
_____
_____
_____
_____
_____

Saturday

Date: _____

_____
_____
_____
_____
_____
_____
_____
_____
_____

Sunday

Date: _____

_____
_____
_____
_____
_____
_____
_____
_____
_____

Additional Thoughts About This Week?

_____
_____
_____
_____
_____
_____
_____
_____

> At the age of 18, I made up my mind to never have another bad day in my life. I dove into a endless sea of gratitude from which I've never emerged.
>
> Patch Adams

Monday

Date: _____

_____
_____
_____
_____
_____
_____
_____
_____
_____

Tuesday

Date: _____

_____
_____
_____
_____
_____
_____
_____
_____

Wednesday

Date: _____

_____
_____
_____
_____
_____
_____
_____
_____
_____

Thursday

Date: _____

_____
_____
_____
_____
_____
_____
_____
_____
_____

Friday

Date: _____

_____
_____
_____
_____
_____
_____
_____
_____
_____

Saturday

Date: _____

_____
_____
_____
_____
_____
_____
_____
_____

Sunday

Date: _____

_____
_____
_____
_____
_____
_____
_____
_____
_____

Additional Thoughts About This Week?

_____
_____
_____
_____
_____
_____
_____
_____

Week 32

Gratitude is one of the strongest and most transformative states of being. It shifts your perspective from lack to abundance and allows you to focus on the good in your life, which in turn pulls more goodness into your reality.

Jen Sincero

Monday

Date: _____

_____
_____
_____
_____
_____
_____
_____
_____
_____

Tuesday

Date: _____

_____
_____
_____
_____
_____
_____
_____
_____
_____

Wednesday

Date: _____

_____
_____
_____
_____
_____
_____
_____
_____
_____

Thursday

Date: _____

_____
_____
_____
_____
_____
_____
_____
_____
_____
_____

Friday

Date: _____

_____
_____
_____
_____
_____
_____
_____
_____
_____

Saturday

Date: _____

_____
_____
_____
_____
_____
_____
_____
_____
_____

Sunday

Date: _____

_____
_____
_____
_____
_____
_____
_____
_____
_____

Additional Thoughts About This Week?

_____
_____
_____
_____
_____
_____
_____
_____

Week 33

I am happy because I'm grateful.
I choose to be grateful.
That gratitude allows me to be happy.
Will Arnett

Monday

Date: _____

_____
_____
_____
_____
_____
_____
_____
_____
_____
_____

Tuesday

Date: _____

_____
_____
_____
_____
_____
_____
_____
_____
_____
_____

Wednesday

Date: _____

_____
_____
_____
_____
_____
_____
_____
_____

Thursday

Date: _____

_____
_____
_____
_____
_____
_____
_____
_____

Friday

Date: _____

_____
_____
_____
_____
_____
_____
_____

Saturday

Date: _____

_____
_____
_____
_____
_____
_____
_____
_____
_____

Sunday

Date: _____

_____
_____
_____
_____
_____
_____
_____
_____
_____
_____

Additional Thoughts About This Week?

_____
_____
_____
_____
_____
_____
_____
_____
_____

When it comes to life the critical thing is whether you take things for granted or take them with gratitude.
Gilbert K. Chesterton

Monday

Date: _____

_____
_____
_____
_____
_____
_____
_____
_____
_____

Tuesday

Date: _____

_____
_____
_____
_____
_____
_____
_____
_____
_____

Wednesday

Date: _____

_____
_____
_____
_____
_____
_____
_____
_____

Thursday

Date: _____

_____
_____
_____
_____
_____
_____
_____
_____
_____

Friday

Date: _____

_____
_____
_____
_____
_____
_____
_____
_____
_____

Saturday

Date: _____

_____
_____
_____
_____
_____
_____
_____
_____
_____
_____

Sunday

Date: _____

_____
_____
_____
_____
_____
_____
_____
_____
_____
_____

Additional Thoughts About This Week?

_____
_____
_____
_____
_____
_____
_____
_____
_____

Week 35

> Live a life full of humility, gratitude,
> intellectual curiosity, and never stop learning.
> Gza

Monday

Date: _____

_____
_____
_____
_____
_____
_____
_____
_____
_____

Tuesday

Date: _____

_____
_____
_____
_____
_____
_____
_____
_____

Wednesday

Date: _____

_____
_____
_____
_____
_____
_____
_____
_____
_____

Thursday

Date: _____

_____
_____
_____
_____
_____
_____
_____
_____
_____
_____
_____

Friday

Date: _____

_____
_____
_____
_____
_____
_____
_____
_____
_____
_____

Saturday

Date: _____

_____
_____
_____
_____
_____
_____
_____
_____
_____
_____

Sunday

Date: _____

_____
_____
_____
_____
_____
_____
_____
_____
_____
_____

Additional Thoughts About This Week?

_____
_____
_____
_____
_____
_____
_____
_____
_____

Week 36

Develop an attitude of gratitude, and give thanks for everything that happens to you, knowing that every step forward is a step toward achieving something bigger and better than your current situation.

Brian Tracy

Monday

Date: _____

_____
_____
_____
_____
_____
_____
_____
_____
_____
_____

Tuesday

Date: _____

_____
_____
_____
_____
_____
_____
_____
_____
_____
_____

Wednesday

Date: _____

_____
_____
_____
_____
_____
_____
_____
_____
_____

Thursday

Date: _____

_____
_____
_____
_____
_____
_____
_____
_____
_____
_____
_____

Friday

Date: _____

_____
_____
_____
_____
_____
_____
_____
_____
_____

Saturday

Date: _____

_____
_____
_____
_____
_____
_____
_____
_____
_____

Sunday

Date: _____

_____
_____
_____
_____
_____
_____
_____
_____
_____
_____

Additional Thoughts About This Week?

_____
_____
_____
_____
_____
_____
_____
_____

Week 37

> *Perhaps nothing helps us make the movement from our little selves to a larger world than remembering God in gratitude. Such a perspective puts God in view in all of life, not just in the moments we set aside for worship or spiritual disciplines. Not just in the moments when life seems easy.* — Henri Nouwen

Monday

Date: _____

_____
_____
_____
_____
_____
_____
_____
_____
_____

Tuesday

Date: _____

_____
_____
_____
_____
_____
_____
_____
_____
_____

Wednesday

Date: _____

_____
_____
_____
_____
_____
_____
_____
_____
_____

Thursday

Date: _____

_____
_____
_____
_____
_____
_____
_____
_____
_____

Friday

Date: _____

_____
_____
_____
_____
_____
_____
_____
_____

Saturday

Date: _____

_____
_____
_____
_____
_____
_____
_____
_____
_____

Sunday

Date: _____

_____
_____
_____
_____
_____
_____
_____
_____
_____
_____

Additional Thoughts About This Week?

_____
_____
_____
_____
_____
_____
_____
_____

Week 38

> When we focus on our gratitude, the tide of
> disappointment goes out and the tide of love rushes in.
>
> Kristin Armstrong

Monday

Date: _____

_____
_____
_____
_____
_____
_____
_____
_____
_____

Tuesday

Date: _____

_____
_____
_____
_____
_____
_____
_____
_____
_____

Wednesday

Date: _____

_____
_____
_____
_____
_____
_____
_____
_____
_____

Thursday

Date: _____

_____
_____
_____
_____
_____
_____
_____
_____
_____
_____
_____
_____

Friday

Date: _____

_____
_____
_____
_____
_____
_____
_____
_____
_____

Saturday

Date: _____

_____

_____

_____

_____

_____

_____

_____

Sunday

Date: _____

_____

_____

_____

_____

_____

_____

_____

Additional Thoughts About This Week?

_____

_____

_____

_____

_____

_____

Week 39

Gratitude is the healthiest of all human emotions.
The more you express gratitude for what you have, the more
likely you will have even more to express gratitude for.

Zig Ziglar

Monday

Date: _____

_____
_____
_____
_____
_____
_____
_____
_____
_____

Tuesday

Date: _____

_____
_____
_____
_____
_____
_____
_____
_____
_____

Wednesday

Date: _____

_____
_____
_____
_____
_____
_____
_____
_____
_____

Thursday

Date: _____

_____
_____
_____
_____
_____
_____
_____
_____
_____
_____

Friday

Date: _____

_____
_____
_____
_____
_____
_____
_____
_____
_____

Saturday

Date: _____

_____
_____
_____
_____
_____
_____
_____
_____

Sunday

Date: _____

_____
_____
_____
_____
_____
_____
_____
_____
_____

Additional Thoughts About This Week?

_____
_____
_____
_____
_____
_____
_____
_____

Week 40

Never lose the childlike wonder.
Show gratitude...
Don't complain; just work harder...
Never give up.
Randy Pausch

Monday

Date: _____

_____
_____
_____
_____
_____
_____
_____
_____
_____
_____

Tuesday

Date: _____

_____
_____
_____
_____
_____
_____
_____
_____
_____
_____

Wednesday

Date: _____

_____
_____
_____
_____
_____
_____
_____
_____
_____

Thursday

Date: _____

_____
_____
_____
_____
_____
_____
_____
_____
_____
_____

Friday

Date: _____

_____
_____
_____
_____
_____
_____
_____
_____
_____

Saturday

Date: _____

_____
_____
_____
_____
_____
_____
_____
_____
_____
_____

Sunday

Date: _____

_____
_____
_____
_____
_____
_____
_____
_____
_____
_____

Additional Thoughts About This Week?

_____
_____
_____
_____
_____
_____
_____
_____
_____

Week 41

> *Feeling gratitude and not expressing it is like wrapping a present and not giving it.*
> *William Arthur Ward*

Monday

Date: _____

_____
_____
_____
_____
_____
_____
_____
_____
_____

Tuesday

Date: _____

_____
_____
_____
_____
_____
_____
_____
_____
_____

Wednesday

Date: _____

_____
_____
_____
_____
_____
_____
_____
_____
_____

Thursday

Date: _____

_____
_____
_____
_____
_____
_____
_____
_____
_____

Friday

Date: _____

_____
_____
_____
_____
_____
_____
_____
_____

Saturday

Date: _____

_____
_____
_____
_____
_____
_____
_____
_____
_____

Sunday

Date: _____

_____
_____
_____
_____
_____
_____
_____
_____
_____

Additional Thoughts About This Week?

_____
_____
_____
_____
_____
_____
_____
_____
_____

Week 42

> Thankfulness is the beginning of gratitude.
> Gratitude is the completion of thankfulness.
> Thankfulness may consist merely of words.
> Gratitude is shown in acts. Henri Frederic Amiel

Monday

Date: _____

_____
_____
_____
_____
_____
_____
_____
_____
_____

Tuesday

Date: _____

_____
_____
_____
_____
_____
_____
_____
_____
_____

Wednesday

Date: _____

_____
_____
_____
_____
_____
_____
_____
_____
_____

Thursday

Date: _____

_____
_____
_____
_____
_____
_____
_____
_____
_____
_____

Friday

Date: _____

_____
_____
_____
_____
_____
_____
_____
_____
_____

Saturday

Date: _____

_____
_____
_____
_____
_____
_____
_____
_____
_____

Sunday

Date: _____

_____
_____
_____
_____
_____
_____
_____
_____
_____

Additional Thoughts About This Week?

_____
_____
_____
_____
_____
_____
_____
_____

> *Give yourself a gift of five minutes of contemplation in awe of everything you see around you. Go outside and turn your attention to the many miracles around you. This five-minute-a-day regimen of appreciation and gratitude will help you to focus your life in awe.*   Wayne Dyer

Monday

Date: _____

_____
_____
_____
_____
_____
_____
_____
_____
_____

Tuesday

Date: _____

_____
_____
_____
_____
_____
_____
_____
_____
_____

Wednesday

Date: _____

_____
_____
_____
_____
_____
_____
_____
_____
_____

Thursday

Date: _____

_____
_____
_____
_____
_____
_____
_____
_____
_____

Friday

Date: _____

_____
_____
_____
_____
_____
_____
_____
_____

Saturday

Date: _____

_____
_____
_____
_____
_____
_____
_____
_____
_____

Sunday

Date: _____

_____
_____
_____
_____
_____
_____
_____
_____
_____
_____

Additional Thoughts About This Week?

_____
_____
_____
_____
_____
_____
_____
_____

> *Joy is the simplest form of gratitude.*
> *Karl Barth*

Monday

Date: _____

_____
_____
_____
_____
_____
_____
_____
_____
_____
_____

Tuesday

Date: _____

_____
_____
_____
_____
_____
_____
_____
_____
_____

Wednesday

Date: _____

_____
_____
_____
_____
_____
_____
_____
_____
_____
_____

Thursday

Date: _____

_____
_____
_____
_____
_____
_____
_____
_____
_____
_____
_____

Friday

Date: _____

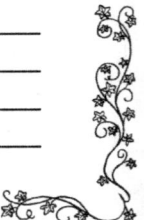

_____
_____
_____
_____
_____
_____
_____
_____
_____

Saturday

Date: _____

_____
_____
_____
_____
_____
_____
_____
_____
_____

Sunday

Date: _____

_____
_____
_____
_____
_____
_____
_____
_____
_____

Additional Thoughts About This Week?

_____
_____
_____
_____
_____
_____
_____
_____

> *Thanksgiving is a time of togetherness and gratitude.*
> *Nigel Hamilton*

Monday

Date: _____

_____
_____
_____
_____
_____
_____
_____
_____
_____

Tuesday

Date: _____

_____
_____
_____
_____
_____
_____
_____
_____
_____

Wednesday

Date: _____

_____
_____
_____
_____
_____
_____
_____
_____
_____
_____

Thursday

Date: _____

_____
_____
_____
_____
_____
_____
_____
_____
_____
_____

Friday

Date: _____

_____
_____
_____
_____
_____
_____
_____
_____
_____

Saturday

Date: _____

_____
_____
_____
_____
_____
_____
_____
_____
_____

Sunday

Date: _____

_____
_____
_____
_____
_____
_____
_____
_____
_____

Additional Thoughts About This Week?

_____
_____
_____
_____
_____
_____
_____
_____

> *Gratitude bestows reverence, allowing us to encounter everyday epiphanies, those transcendent moments of awe that change forever how we experience life and the world.*
> *John Milton*

Monday

Date: _____

_____
_____
_____
_____
_____
_____
_____
_____
_____
_____

Tuesday

Date: _____

_____
_____
_____
_____
_____
_____
_____
_____
_____
_____

Wednesday

Date: _____

_____

_____

_____

_____

_____

_____

_____

_____

Thursday

Date: _____

_____

_____

_____

_____

_____

_____

_____

_____

_____

_____

Friday

Date: _____

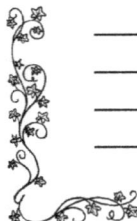

_____

_____

_____

_____

_____

_____

_____

_____

Saturday

Date: _____

_____
_____
_____
_____
_____
_____
_____
_____
_____

Sunday

Date: _____

_____
_____
_____
_____
_____
_____
_____
_____
_____

Additional Thoughts About This Week?

_____
_____
_____
_____
_____
_____
_____
_____
_____

Week 47

> *The essence of all beautiful art, all great art, is gratitude.*
> *Friedrich Nietzsche*

Monday

Date: _____

_____

_____

_____

_____

_____

_____

_____

Tuesday

Date: _____

_____

_____

_____

_____

_____

_____

_____

_____

Wednesday

Date: _____

_____
_____
_____
_____
_____
_____
_____
_____
_____

Thursday

Date: _____

_____
_____
_____
_____
_____
_____
_____
_____
_____

Friday

Date: _____

_____
_____
_____
_____
_____
_____
_____
_____
_____

Saturday

Date: _____

_____
_____
_____
_____
_____
_____
_____
_____
_____

Sunday

Date: _____

_____
_____
_____
_____
_____
_____
_____
_____
_____

Additional Thoughts About This Week?

_____
_____
_____
_____
_____
_____
_____
_____

Week 48

> *Gratitude is the most exquisite form of courtesy.*
> Jacques Maritain

Monday

Date: _____

_____
_____
_____
_____
_____
_____
_____
_____
_____

Tuesday

Date: _____

_____
_____
_____
_____
_____
_____
_____
_____
_____

Wednesday

Date: _____

_____
_____
_____
_____
_____
_____
_____
_____
_____

Thursday

Date: _____

_____
_____
_____
_____
_____
_____
_____
_____
_____
_____
_____

Friday

Date: _____

_____
_____
_____
_____
_____
_____
_____
_____
_____

Saturday

Date: _____

_____
_____
_____
_____
_____
_____
_____
_____
_____
_____

Sunday

Date: _____

_____
_____
_____
_____
_____
_____
_____
_____
_____
_____

Additional Thoughts About This Week?

_____
_____
_____
_____
_____
_____
_____
_____

Week 49

> *Have gratitude for all that you have,*
> *and you can be happy exactly as you are.*
> *Mandy Ingber*

Monday

Date: _____

_____
_____
_____
_____
_____
_____
_____
_____
_____

Tuesday

Date: _____

_____
_____
_____
_____
_____
_____
_____
_____
_____

Wednesday

Date: _____

_____

_____

_____

_____

_____

_____

_____

_____

_____

Thursday

Date: _____

_____

_____

_____

_____

_____

_____

_____

_____

_____

_____

Friday

Date: _____

_____

_____

_____

_____

_____

_____

_____

_____

_____

Saturday

Date: _____

_____

_____

_____

_____

_____

_____

_____

_____

_____

_____

Sunday

Date: _____

_____

_____

_____

_____

_____

_____

_____

_____

_____

_____

Additional Thoughts About This Week?

_____

_____

_____

_____

_____

_____

_____

_____

_____

Week 50

Gratitude can transform common days into thanksgivings, turn routine jobs into joy, and change ordinary opportunities into blessings.
William Arthur Ward

Monday

Date: _____

_____
_____
_____
_____
_____
_____
_____
_____
_____

Tuesday

Date: _____

_____
_____
_____
_____
_____
_____
_____
_____

Wednesday   Date: _____

_____
_____
_____
_____
_____
_____
_____
_____
_____
_____

Thursday   Date: _____

_____
_____
_____
_____
_____
_____
_____
_____
_____
_____
_____
_____

Friday   Date: _____

_____
_____
_____
_____
_____
_____
_____
_____
_____
_____
_____

Saturday

Date: _____

_____
_____
_____
_____
_____
_____
_____
_____
_____

Sunday

Date: _____

_____
_____
_____
_____
_____
_____
_____
_____
_____
_____

Additional Thoughts About This Week?

_____
_____
_____
_____
_____
_____
_____
_____

> *What will you and I give for Christmas this year? Let us in our lives give to our Lord and Savior the gift of gratitude by living His teachings and following in His footsteps.*
>
> Thomas S. Monson

Monday

Date: _____

_____
_____
_____
_____
_____
_____
_____
_____
_____

Tuesday

Date: _____

_____
_____
_____
_____
_____
_____
_____
_____
_____

Wednesday

Date: _____

_____
_____
_____
_____
_____
_____
_____
_____

Thursday

Date: _____

_____
_____
_____
_____
_____
_____
_____
_____
_____
_____

Friday

Date: _____

_____
_____
_____
_____
_____
_____
_____
_____

Saturday

Date: _____

_____
_____
_____
_____
_____
_____
_____
_____
_____
_____

Sunday

Date: _____

_____
_____
_____
_____
_____
_____
_____
_____
_____
_____

Additional Thoughts About This Week?

_____
_____
_____
_____
_____
_____
_____
_____
_____

Week 52

> Gratitude makes sense of our past, brings peace for today,
> and creates a vision for tomorrow.
> Melody Beattie

Monday

Date: _____

_____
_____
_____
_____
_____
_____
_____
_____
_____

Tuesday

Date: _____

_____
_____
_____
_____
_____
_____
_____
_____
_____

Wednesday

Date: _____

_____
_____
_____
_____
_____
_____
_____
_____

Thursday

Date: _____

_____
_____
_____
_____
_____
_____
_____
_____
_____
_____

Friday

Date: _____

_____
_____
_____
_____
_____
_____
_____
_____
_____

Saturday

Date: _____

_____
_____
_____
_____
_____
_____
_____
_____
_____

Sunday

Date: _____

_____
_____
_____
_____
_____
_____
_____
_____
_____
_____

Additional Thoughts About This Week?

_____
_____
_____
_____
_____
_____
_____
_____

Week 53

Have gratitude for all that you have,
and you can be happy exactly as you are.
Mandy Ingber

Monday

Date: _____

_____
_____
_____
_____
_____
_____
_____
_____
_____

Tuesday

Date: _____

_____
_____
_____
_____
_____
_____
_____
_____
_____

Wednesday

Date: _____

_____

_____

_____

_____

_____

_____

_____

_____

_____

Thursday

Date: _____

_____

_____

_____

_____

_____

_____

_____

_____

_____

Friday

Date: _____

_____

_____

_____

_____

_____

_____

_____

_____

Saturday

Date: _____

_____
_____
_____
_____
_____
_____
_____
_____

Sunday

Date: _____

_____
_____
_____
_____
_____
_____
_____
_____

Additional Thoughts About This Week?

_____
_____
_____
_____
_____
_____
_____
_____

Week 54

> *Gratitude is when memory is stored*
> *in the heart and not in the mind.*
> Lionel Hampton

Monday

Date: _____

_____
_____
_____
_____
_____
_____
_____
_____
_____

Tuesday

Date: _____

_____
_____
_____
_____
_____
_____
_____
_____

Wednesday

Date: _____

_____
_____
_____
_____
_____
_____
_____
_____
_____

Thursday

Date: _____

_____
_____
_____
_____
_____
_____
_____
_____
_____

Friday

Date: _____

_____
_____
_____
_____
_____
_____
_____
_____
_____

Saturday

Date: _____

_____
_____
_____
_____
_____
_____
_____
_____
_____

Sunday

Date: _____

_____
_____
_____
_____
_____
_____
_____
_____
_____

Additional Thoughts About This Week?

_____
_____
_____
_____
_____
_____
_____
_____

So, how has your gratitude journey been? Did you find that your life is full of things for which you are grateful?

I hope you can see all the wonderful blessings you enjoy every day.

I would love to hear from you, especially if you found this journal beneficial to your growth.

You can contact me at dianneter@gmail.com.

Be sure to check out my other books available on Amazon.

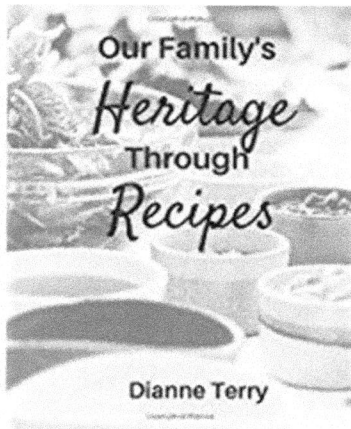

My
Bible Study
Journal

Part of the Journey Series

Dianne Terry

My Pocket
Prayer List
Journal
Part of the Journey Series

Dianne Terry

My
Prayer
Journal

Part of the Journey Series

Dianne Terry

Our Family's
Heritage
Through
Recipes

Dianne Terry

www.ingramcontent.com/pod-product-compliance
Lightning Source LLC
Chambersburg PA
CBHW081647270326
41933CB00018B/3371